leaflets three, let it be!

the story of poison ivy

Anita Sanchez   Illustrated by Robin Brickman

BOYDS MILLS PRESS

AN IMPRINT OF HIGHLIGHTS

Honesdale, Pennsylvania

Winter woods are dark. Bare branches rattle in the icy wind.

A thick brown vine creeps up a tree. Shaggy rootlets help it cling to the bark.

The vine curls through the branches like a furry snake.

Hairy vine—a warning sign!

One cold day in early spring, buds on the vine pop open. Baby leaves unfold, shiny and red as a traffic light.

Stop!

If you touch the leaves, they might make you itch.

Meet poison ivy!

Poison ivy isn't poisonous like a
rattlesnake or a black widow spider.
A chemical in the sap, *urushiol*,
might give you an itchy rash.

A rabbit hops down the path. He's thin and hungry after a hard winter. Few leaves are growing yet—not much to eat. He nibbles tender leaflets of poison ivy.

Snort! A hungry doe scares him away. Then she snacks on the leaves, while . . .

Squeak! White-footed mice gnaw on poison ivy stems, until . . .

Growl! A cranky bear, woken from his long sleep, wants a bite, too.

Tender red leaves are the first taste of spring. But poison ivy has more to give.

In summer, the red leaves fade to green. They hide among other plants. Look closely!

Can you identify poison ivy?
Like snowflakes, no two poison ivy
leaves are exactly alike.
Each leaf is divided into three *leaflets*.
Some are jagged or toothed. Some are
smooth-edged. Some are the size of a
dime, others bigger than your hand.
Look for the "head" (*middle leaflet*)
on a long neck (*stem*).
Twin side leaflets have short stems.
Sometimes little mitten thumbs stick
out. (Don't shake hands.)

Leaflets three, let it be!

Sun and rain make poison ivy grow strong. Vines creep up the tree and leaves spread over the ground at ankle-height. Watch where you step!

The leaves shade the forest floor like a million green umbrellas. In their cool, moist shadows, salamanders wriggle and spiders spin webs. A golden-eyed toad watches for insect prey.

Swooping low, a cardinal carries food to hungry babies. They're cradled safely under a tangle of vines, in a nest lined with poison ivy rootlets.

Dainty flowers hang in clusters from the hairy vine.
   Bees hum and buzz among the blossoms, gathering
poison ivy nectar to make into golden honey.
   Shade and sweetness in the hottest days of summer . . .
but poison ivy has more to give.

Fall days grow short and chilly. Tiny insects roll themselves up in snug poison ivy blankets.

Aphids, beetles, and caterpillars crunch and munch on poison ivy leaves. Leaf miners tunnel through, eating as they go.

Leaves glow scarlet, orange, purple, gold—
a poison ivy rainbow!
    And, hidden under bright leaves, tiny berries
are slowly ripening.
    Poison ivy has still more to give.

Winter comes. Withered leaves fall to the ground.
Empty branches rattle in a cold sky.
The forest seems barren.
But the hairy vine is loaded with plump white berries.

Berries white, take flight!

Hungry birds flock to a poison ivy feast.
A red-bellied woodpecker hangs upside down from the vine, grabbing the white berries. A wild turkey gobbles them up, too. Chickadees flit from branch to branch. Robins and bluebirds join in.

The hairy vine is a living bird feeder.

Poison ivy gives life in the starving heart of winter.

The cold is almost done. As winter fades, poison
ivy seedlings sprout.
    Hairy vines reach for the sun.
    Leaflets three shine red to welcome spring!

Itching To Know More?

How does touching a plant make me itchy?

Poison ivy contains an oily chemical called urushiol. If you touch any part of the plant—leaves, berries, roots, or stems—this oil can get onto your skin. And if you're allergic to urushiol, you might develop an itchy rash. (No urushiol is in the nectar, so the honey won't make anyone itchy.)

Approximately eighty-five percent of people are allergic to poison ivy. Usually you won't get a rash the first time you touch the plant—but your body may be sensitized to it, and you might get a rash next time.

Can I get itchy from walking by poison ivy?

No, you have to get the oil directly on your skin. You might get it from clothes or pets that have touched poison ivy.

Will it hurt if I touch poison ivy?

Not a bit. It's not like being stung by an angry wasp or pricked by a thorny thistle. Most people never even notice poison ivy as they walk through it.

At first, nothing happens. It usually takes a day or so for a red-colored rash to develop. Blisters may pop up, too. And then it gets itchy!

What should I do if I've touched poison ivy?

Wash off the oil as soon as possible. Use lots of cool water—soap isn't necessary. If you're far from a sink, rinse off in a stream, or go swimming.

Oh, no! I'm starting to itch. What can I do?

Don't scratch! Scratching makes skin sore. Calamine lotion or other over-the-counter remedies might help. Check with your doctor for more advice.

The rash usually lasts about two weeks and goes away by itself. Call the doctor if the rash persists or is causing much discomfort.

My friends at school won't sit next to me. Will I give them the rash?

No, poison ivy is not contagious.

I scratched too much, and now it's spreading!

No urushiol is contained in the blisters, so scratching doesn't spread the irritation. Some areas of the rash may show up later than others. Or maybe you touched something else that had urushiol on it, like the shoes you wore in the woods.

How can birds and other animals eat poison ivy? Don't their mouths get itchy?

Poison ivy can make humans itch, but it doesn't harm the forest animals who depend on it. No one knows why humans are allergic to this plant.

Poison ivy only grows in the forest, right?

Poison ivy can grow almost anywhere. It's found throughout North America, lurking in shady forests or sunny meadows. It can grow on the edges of parking lots, or among sand dunes on a beach. Or in your backyard.

I don't want poison ivy in my backyard! How can I get rid of it?

Work with an adult to find safe ways. Try spreading black plastic over the plants, and leave the plastic down for six months. Wear heavy, disposable gloves. Never burn poison ivy—smoke carrying urushiol droplets can damage your lungs.

Think carefully before using an *herbicide*. Herbicides are poisons that kill unwanted plants, but their powerful chemicals can harm people's health. Herbicides can hurt animals, too—dogs, cats, birds, frogs, butterflies, and more.

Why does such a bad plant exist?

Plants aren't "bad" or "good." They just are! Poison ivy is native to this continent—it was here long before people were. Poison ivy gives abundant food and shelter to wildlife, and helps prevent soil erosion, too.

It can make people itchy—but it's an important plant. Poison ivy has a place to fill, a job to do.

Poison Ivy Look-Alikes

Some plants are often mistaken for poison ivy. Below are leaves from four plants:

A Poison Ivy (*Toxicodendron radicans*)
B Wild Strawberry (*Fragaria virginiana*)
C Virginia Creeper (*Parthenocissus quinquefolia*)
D Wild Raspberry (*Rubus spp.*)

Which of these plants are poison ivy?

(Answers are on the next page.)

To George, who watched the woodpeckers
at their poison ivy feast
—AS

For Jennie and Jared: Wander and wonder,
but watch where you walk!
—RB

Text copyright © 2014 by Anita Sanchez
Illustrations copyright © 2014 by Robin Brickman
All rights reserved
For information about permission to reproduce selections
from this book, contact permissions@highlights.com.

Boyds Mills Press
An Imprint of Highlights
815 Church Street
Honesdale, Pennsylvania 18431

Printed in China
ISBN: 978-1-62091-445-8
Library of Congress Control Number: 2014943962

First edition
10 9 8 7 6 5 4 3 2 1

Design by Barbara Grzeslo
Production by Margaret Mosomillo
The text of this book is set in Billy.

Artist's Note

I created the artwork for this book with watercolors and acrylic paints on paper, cutting and shaping the painted paper by hand, and gluing it in place. The only parts of the illustrations that aren't made of paper are: glue-gun drips for water droplets, sewing thread or human hair for spider webs and whiskers, and clear plastic from a pasta box window for insect wings. I used no found elements from nature. The three-dimensional paintings were photographed to produce the images for this book. —RB

Answer key to Poison Ivy Look-Alikes
A Poison Ivy (*Toxicodendron radicans*)
B Wild Strawberry (*Fragaria virginiana*)
C Virginia Creeper (*Parthenocissus quinquefolia*)
D Wild Raspberry (*Rubus spp.*)